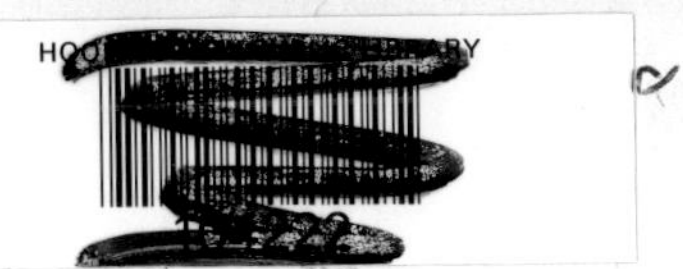

DATE DUE

JUN 2 0 1980	DEC 2 7 1980	
JUL 1 1980	JUL 8 1991	
DEC 2 2 1980	AUG 0 3	
JUN 2 3 1981	NOV 2 8 1995	
JUL 2 8 1981	AUG 0 2	
MAR 1 8 1982		
AUG 1 1 1982		
MAY 3 1 1983		
JAN 2 3 1986		
FEB 6 1986		
AUG 5 1987		

J
796.323   Paige, David
PAI   Pro basketball: an almanac
          of facts and records

MAN, WILT CHAMBERLAIN HOLDS MORE SCORING RECORDS IN THIS BOOK THAN ANYONE ELSE!!
Hey! What's Shakin'?
IT COULDN'T BE HELPED KIDS. HUSTLE, YA KNOW.

BASKETBALL FACTS STATIS...

PRO BASKETBALL SINCE T...

BY DAVID PAIGE/CREATIVE E...

Basketball

TICS AND RECORDS ABOUT
HE BEGINNING (DUNK IT!)
UCATION/CHILDRENS PRESS

CONTENTS

THE SPORT 6

THE PLAYERS 20

The team listed for a player is either the team he was most associated with or the team that he was presently associated with when a particular record was set or a specific event took place.

PHOTO CREDITS

UPI..........cover, 15, 35, 36, 37 (Mikan), 37 (Russell), 39 (Pettit)
Vernon J. Biever..........6, 27
Ronald C. Modra..........11, 20, 29, 33, 38 (Frazier), 38 (DeBusschere)
Bruce Curtis..........19, 22, 30, 38 (Havlicek)
Peter Travers/Bruce Curtis..........39 (Auerbach)

ILLUSTRATIONS

John Keely..........5, 8, 9, 10, 11

Cover: Dr. James Naismith, inventor of basketball, and the first Basketball team in 1891.

Published by Creative Educational Society, Inc., 123 South Broad Street, Mankato, Minnesota 56001. Copyright © 1977 by Creative Educational Society, Inc. International copyrights reserved in all countries. No part of this book may be reproduced in any form without written permission from the publisher. Printed in the United States.

Library of Congress Cataloging in Publication Data

Paige, David.
  Pro basketball.
  SUMMARY: An illustrated almanac of basketball facts and records such as top scorers and player making the most free throws.
  1. Basketball—United States—Records—Juvenile literature. [1. Basketball—Records]   I. Title.
GV885.55.P34   796.33′2′0973   77-2547
ISBN 0-87191-605-3

the
sport

The Story of Basket ball

A game somewhat like basketball was played by the Aztec Indians in Mexico in the 1500's, according to the Guinness Book of Sports' Records. But it was different.

The object was to put a rubber ball through a stone ring situated high on a wall of the stadium. If a player succeeded in doing that, he was (again according to Guinness) entitled to the clothing of all the spectators. And the captain of the losing team was often beheaded.

The game of basketball that we know today, however, is a true American creation. It was invented here more than 80 years ago. In the beginning, a peach basket perched on the top of a pole was used. Teams, in those days, might have as few as three players each; on the other hand they might also have as many as 40 players on a side.

Basketball has, of course, changed over the years. Today it is one of the most popular sports in the world, played indoors and outdoors by thousands of people and watched in person and on television by millions of others.

The following is a brief history of the exciting sport of basketball.

The game of basketball is invented by Dr. James Naismith in Springfield, Massachusetts.

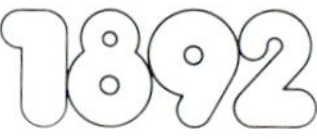

The first basketball team — the International YMCA Training School (later to become Springfield College) — is organized by Dr. James Naismith in Springfield, Massachusetts.

The first official basketball game is held at Springfield between Central YMCA and Armory Hill YMCA. It ends in a 2 – 2 tie.

The first girl's basketball game is held in Springfield, but the teams are not organized.

The first college basketball team is turned out at Vanderbilt University, Nashville, Tennessee.

The official modern scoring system of two points for a field goal and one point for a free throw is established.

The first intercollegiate game is held in Minnesota: Minnesota State School of Agriculture defeats Hamline College 9 – 3.

The first professional game is played at Trenton, New Jersey with local players but no organized teams.

An official basketball rules committee is established.

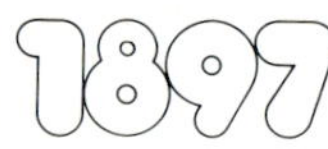

The first modern intercollegiate game between two teams of five players each is played: Yale defeats the University of Pennsylvania 32 – 10.

The first Amateur Athletic Union (AAU) national tournament is held in New York City (won by 23rd Street YMCA).

The National Basketball League (NBL), the first professional basketball association, is established in Philadelphia, Pennsylvania.

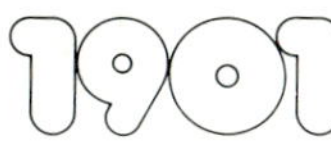

The first collegiate basketball league, called the Eastern League, is organized with five teams. Yale is the first league champion.

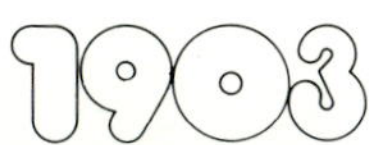

The NBL folds and is replaced by another professional association called the Philadelphia League.

The Philadelphia League changes its name to the Eastern League.

The first of the great professional teams, the Original Celtics, is formed in New York City.

Abe Saperstein founds the Harlem Globetrotters.

The first national AAU championships in women's basketball are held at Pasadena, California. Winning team is the Pasadena Athletic & Country Club.

The first college All-America team is selected.

The first college double-header is held at Madison Square Garden in New York (New York University 25 – Notre Dame 18, Westminster College 37 – St. John's 33).

Basketball is added as a competition to the Olympic Games. In Berlin, Germany, the United States wins the first Olympic championship, defeating Canada 19 – 8.

A new professional National Basketball League (NBL) is formed.

The laceless basketball is introduced and accepted as the standard ball.

The first national college tournament is conducted by the National Association of Intercollegiate Athletics (NAIA) in New York City.

The National Invitational Tournament (NIT) is organized and holds its first national tourney in New York City.

The National Collegiate Athletic Association (NCAA) conducts its first national championship tournament.

The first modern professional basketball league, the Basketball Association of America (BAA) is established.

The Boston Celtics, New York Knickerbockers and the Philadelphia Warriors (today the Golden State Warriors) are charter members of the BAA.

The Minneapolis Lakers (now the Los Angeles Lakers), the Fort Wayne Pistons (today the Detroit Pistons) and the Rochester Royals (today the Kansas City Kings) join the BAA.

The BAA and the older NBL merge to form the 17-team National Basketball Association (NBA).

The first NBA president is Maurice Podoloff.

The St. Louis Hawks (today the Atlanta Hawks) and the Syracuse Nationals (now the Philadelphia 76ers) join the NBA.

The Minneapolis Lakers become the first team to win three consecutive NBA championships.

The Boston Celtics set an all-time record of scoring 173 points in one game (defeating the Minneapolis Lakers).

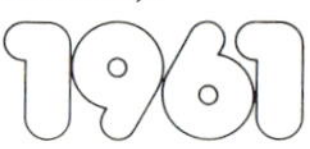

The Baltimore Bullets (today the Washington Bullets) join the NBA.

1962

Wilt Chamberlain of the Philadelphia Warriors scores 100 points in one game as Philadelphia defeats the New York Knickerbockers 169 – 147.

1966

Bill Russell becomes the first black head coach in the NBA (Boston Celtics).

The Chicago Bulls become a member of the NBA.

The Boston Celtics win their 8th consecutive NBA championship.

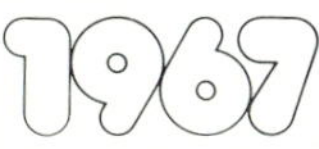

1967

The American Basketball Association (ABA) is founded with 11 teams. George Mikan is named the first ABA commissioner.

The Seattle Supersonics and the San Diego Rockets (today the Houston Rockets) join the NBA.

1968

The James Naismith Basketball Hall of Fame is established at Springfield, Massachusetts.

The Milwaukee Bucks and the Phoenix Suns join the NBA.

1970

The Buffalo Braves, Cleveland Cavaliers and Portland Trail Blazers become members of the NBA.

1974

The New Orleans Jazz joins the NBA.

1976

The American Basketball Association (ABA) folds.

Four former ABA teams join the NBA: Denver Nuggets, Indiana Pacers, New York Nets and San Antonio Spurs.

The Philadelphia 76ers pay $6,000,000 for a player, Julius Erving ($3,000,000 goes to player and $3,000,000 to New York Nets who held his contract).

BILL RUSSELL

Hall of Fame

(Located in Springfield, Massachusetts)

Player	Team Association
Elgin Baylor	Seattle U-Los Angeles Lakers
John Beckman	Original Celtics
Bennie Borgmann	Early pro teams
Joe Brennan	Early pro teams
Bob Cousy	Holy Cross U. – Boston Celtics
Bob Davies	Seton Hall U. – Rochester Royals
Forrest DeBernardi	Westminster College – AAU
Henry (Dutch) Dehnert	Original Celtics
Paul Endacott	U. of Kansas
Bud Foster	U. of Wisconsin – Early pro teams
Marty Friedman	Early pro teams
Lauren Gale	U. of Oregon
Tom Gola	LaSalle U. — Philadelphia Warriors
Robert (Ace) Gruenig	AAU
Victor Hanson	Syracuse U. – Cleveland Rosenblums
Nat Holman	Original Celtics
Chuck Hyatt	U. of Pittsburgh – AAU
William Johnson	AAU
Ed (Moose) Krause	U. of Notre Dame
Bob Kurland	Oklahoma State U. – AAU
Joe Lapchick	Original Celtics
Hank Luisetti	Stanford U.
Ed Macauley	St. Louis U. – Boston Celtics
Branch McCracken	U. of Indiana
Jack McCracken	Northwest Missouri State U. – AAU
George Mikan	DePaul U. – Minneapolis Lakers
Charles (Stretch) Murphy	Purdue U.
Pat Page	U. of Chicago
Bob Pettit	L.S.U. – St. Louis Hawks
Andy Phillip	U. of Illinois – Chicago Stags
John Roosma	U.S. Military Academy
Bill Russell	U. of San Francisco – Boston Celtics
John (Honey) Russell	New York U. – Early pro teams
Dolph Schayes	New York U. – Syracuse Nationals
Ernest Schmidt	Kansas State College
John Schommer	U. of Chicago
Barney Sedran	C.C.N.Y. – Early pro teams
Bill Sharman	U. of Southern California – Boston Celtics

Christian Steinmetz	U. of Wisconsin
John (Cat) Thompson	Montana State U.
Bob (Fuzzy) Vandivier	Franklin College (Indiana)
Edward Wachter	Early pro teams
John Wooden	Purdue U.

*The Hall of Fame honors those who have contributed to basketball on the professional, college and AAU levels of competition.

Coach	Team Association
Arnold (Red) Auerbach	Boston Celtics
Ernest Blood	High Schools (New York, New Jersey) – U.S. Military Academy
Tarzan Cooper	New York Renaissance
Howard Cann	New York U.
Clifford Carlson	U. of Pittsburgh
Ben Carnevale	U.S. Naval Academy
Everett Dean	U. of Indiana – Stanford U.
Edgar Dibble	Western Kentucky U.
Bruce Drake	U. of Oklahoma
Amory (Slats) Gill	Oregon State U.
Howard Hobson	U. of Oregon – Yale U.
Hank Iba	Oklahoma State U.
Alvin (Doggie) Julian	Holy Cross U. – Dartmouth U. – Boston Celtics
Frank Keaney	U. of Rhode Island
George Keogan	U. of Notre Dame
Ward Lambert	Purdue U.
Harry Litwack	Temple U.
Kenneth Loeffler	LaSalle U.
Arthur (Dutch) Lonborg	Northwestern U.
Frank McGuire	U of South Carolina
Walter Meanwell	U. of Wisconsin
Adolph Rupp	U. of Kentucky
Leonard Sachs	Loyola U. (Chicago)
John Wooden	U.C.L.A.

Contributor	Basketball Association
Forrest (Phog) Allen	Founder, National Assn. of Basketball Coaches
Clair Bee	Coach and Organizer
Walter Brown	Founder, NBA
John Bunn	Coach and Basketball Writer
Bob Douglas	Team Founder, the Renaissance (Rens)
Harry Fischer	Rules Organizer
Ed Gottlieb	Organizer and Team Owner
Luther Gulick	Sport Organizer
Edward Hickox	Sport and Rules Organizer
Tony Hinkle	Coach and Organizer
Ned Irish	Organizer and Director of Madison Square Garden
William Jones	International Organizer
Emil Liston	Coach and Organizer
Bill Mokray	Promoter and Writer
Ralph Morgan	Founder, Rules Committee

Contributor	Basketball Association
Frank Morgenweck	Promoter
James Naismith	Inventor of the Game
John O'Brien	Organizer and Administrator
Harold Olsen	Coach and Organizer
Maurice Podoloff	Organizer and Administrator
H. V. Porter	Administrator and Rules Organizer
William Reid	Athletic Director and Administrator
Elmer Ripley	Player, Coach, Organizer
Lynn St. John	Administrator and Rules Organizer
Abe Saperstein	Founder, Harlem Globetrotters
Art Schabinger	Coach and Rules Organizer
Amos Alonzo Stagg	Coach and Organizer
Chuck Taylor	Organizer and Promoter
Oswald Tower	Rules Organizer and Referee
Arthur Trester	Administrator and Organizer
Clifford Wells	Coach, Administrator, Writer

BOB COUSY (14)

The NBA Today

Western Conference

		Colors	Stadium
Midwest Division	Chicago Bulls	Red, White & Black	Chicago Stadium
	Denver Nuggets	Red, White & Blue	McNichols Sports Arena
	Detroit Pistons	Red, White & Blue	Cobo Arena
	Indiana Pacers	Blue & Gold	Market Square Arena
	Kansas City Kings	Red, White & Blue	Kemper Memorial Arena & Omaha Civic Center
	Milwaukee Bucks	Green, Red & White	Milwaukee Arena
Pacific Division	Golden State Warriors	Gold & Blue	Oakland Coliseum
	Los Angeles Lakers	Blue & Gold	The Forum
	Phoenix Suns	Purple, Orange & Copper	Veterans Memorial Coliseum
	Portland Trail Blazers	Scarlet, Black & White	Memorial Coliseum
	Seattle Supersonics	Green & Gold	Seattle Center Coliseum

Eastern Conference

		Colors	Stadium
Atlantic Division	Boston Celtics	Green & White	Boston Gardens & Hartford Civic Center
	Buffalo Braves	Blue & White	Memorial Auditorium
	New York Knickerbockers	Blue, Orange & White	Madison Square Garden
	New York Nets	White, Red & Blue	Nassau Veterans Memorial Coliseum
	Philadelphia 76ers	Red, White & Blue	The Spectrum
Central Division	Atlanta Hawks	Red & White	The Omni
	Cleveland Cavaliers	Wine & Gold	The Coliseum
	Houston Rockets	Red & Gold	The Summit
	New Orleans Jazz	Purple, Green & Gold	Louisiana Superdome
	San Antonio Spurs	Silver & Black	Hemis Fair Arena
	Washington Bullets	Red, White & Blue	Capital Centre

NBA Champions

The NBA Champions

Season	Team	Playoffs (games)
1975–76	Boston Celtics	(4–2, over Phoenix Suns)
1974–75	Golden State Warriors	(4–0, over Washington Bullets)
1973–74	Boston Celtics	(4–3, over Milwaukee Bucks)
1972–73	New York Knickerbockers	(4–1, over Los Angeles Lakers)
1971–72	Los Angeles Lakers	(4–1, over New York Knickerbockers)
1970–71	Milwaukee Bucks	(4–0, over Baltimore Bullets)
1969–70	New York Knickerbockers	(4–3, over Los Angeles Lakers)
1968–69	Boston Celtics	(4–3, over Los Angeles Lakers)
1967–68	Boston Celtics	(4–2, over Los Angeles Lakers)
1966–67	Philadelphia 76ers	(4–2, over San Francisco Warriors)
1965–66	Boston Celtics	(4–3, over Los Angeles Lakers)
1964–65	Boston Celtics	(4–1, over Los Angeles Lakers)
1963–64	Boston Celtics	(4–1, over San Francisco Warriors)
1962–63	Boston Celtics	(4–2, over Los Angeles Lakers)
1961–62	Boston Celtics	(4–2, over Detroit Pistons)
1960–61	Boston Celtics	(4–1, over St. Louis Hawks)
1959–60	Boston Celtics	(4–3, over St. Louis Hawks)
1958–59	Boston Celtics	(4–0, over Minneapolis Lakers)
1957–58	St. Louis Hawks	(4–2, over Boston Celtics)
1956–57	Boston Celtics	(4–3, over St. Louis Hawks)
1955–56	Philadelphia Warriors	(4–1, over Fort Wayne Pistons)
1954–55	Syracuse Nationals	(4–3, over Fort Wayne Pistons)
1953–54	Minncapolis Lakers	(4–3, over Syracuse Nationals)
1952–53	Minneapolis Lakers	(4–1, over New York Knickerbockers)
1951–52	Minneapolis Lakers	(4–3, over New York Knickerbockers)
1950–51	Rochester Royals	(4–3, over New York Knickerbockers)
1949–50	Minneapolis Lakers	(4–2, over Syracuse Nationals)
1948–49	Minneapolis Lakers	(4–2, over Washington Capitols)
1947–48	Baltimore Bullets	(4–2, over Philadelphia Warriors)
1946–47	Philadelphia Warriors	(4–1, over Chicago Stags)

BOSTON
CELTICS
1974
WORLD
CHAMPIONS
BOSTON
CELTICS
BOSTON
CELTICS
BOSTON
CELTICS
BOSTON
CELTICS
CELTICS
30
BUFFALO
BUFFALO
24
BUFFALO
15
SMITH
9
27
33

the
players

All-Around Scorers

The Top 10 Scorers of All-Time

	Team	Total Points	No. of Field Goals	No. of Free Throws	Average Points Per Game
Wilt Chamberlain	Philadelphia	31,419	12,681	6,057	30.1
Oscar Robertson	Milwaukee	26,710	9,508	7,694	25.7
Jerry West	Los Angeles	25,192	9,016	7,160	27.0
John Havlicek	Boston	23,678	9,387	4,904	21.4
Elgin Baylor	Los Angeles	23,149	8,693	5,763	27.4
Hal Greer	Philadelphia	21,586	8,504	4,578	19.2
Walt Bellamy	New York	20,941	7,914	5,113	20.1
Bob Pettit	St. Louis	20,880	7,349	6,182	26.4
Dolph Schayes	Syracuse	19,249	6,135	6,979	18.2
Chet Walker	Chicago	18,831	6,876	5,079	18.2

Top Scoring in a Season

	Team	Total Points	No. of Field Goals	No. of Free Throws	Season
Wilt Chamberlain	Philadelphia	4,029	1,597	835	1961–62
Wilt Chamberlain	San Francisco	3,586	1,463	660	1962–63
Wilt Chamberlain	Philadelphia	3,033	1,251	531	1960–61
Wilt Chamberlain	San Francisco	2,948	1,204	540	1963–64
Bob McAdoo	Buffalo	2,831	1,095	641	1974–75

Top Scoring in a Game

	Team	Total Points	Field Goals	Free Throws	Game
Wilt Chamberlain	Philadelphia	100	36	28	vs. New York, Mar. 2, 1962
Wilt Chamberlain	Philadelphia	78	31	16	vs. Los Angeles, Dec. 8, 1961
Wilt Chamberlain	San Francisco	73	29	15	vs. New York, Nov. 16, 1962
Wilt Chamberlain	Philadelphia	73	29	15	vs. Chicago, Jan. 13, 1962
Wilt Chamberlain	San Francisco	72	29	14	vs. Los Angeles Nov. 3, 1962
Elgin Baylor	Los Angeles	71	28	15	vs. New York, Nov. 15, 1960

The Best Scoring Averages of All-Time

	Team	Average Points Per Game	No. of Games Played
Wilt Chamberlain	Philadelphia	30.1	1,045
Kareem Abdul-Jabbar	Los Angeles	30.0	549
Elgin Baylor	Los Angeles	27.4	846
Jerry West	Los Angeles	27.0	932
Rick Barry	Golden State	26.7	481

Best Scoring Averages in a Season

	Team	Average Points Per Game	No. of Games Played	Season
Wilt Chamberlain	Philadelphia	50.4	80	1961–62
Wilt Chamberlain	San Francisco	44.8	80	1962–63
Wilt Chamberlain	Philadelphia	38.4	79	1960–61
Wilt Chamberlain	Philadelphia	37.6	72	1959–60
Wilt Chamberlain	San Francisco	36.9	80	1963–64

Most Times Leading League in Scoring

	Team	No. of Seasons	Seasons
Wilt Chamberlain	Philadelphia	7	1959–66
Bob McAdoo	Buffalo	3	1973–76
Kareem Abdul-Jabbar	Milwaukee	3	1969–72
Neil Johnston	Philadelphia	3	1952–55
George Mikan	Minneapolis	3	1948–51

Most Seasons Scoring 1,000 or More Points

	Team	No. of Seasons	Seasons
John Havlicek	Boston	14	1962–76
Jerry West	Los Angeles	13	1961–73
Oscar Robertson	Cincinnati	13	1961–73
Wilt Chamberlain	Philadelphia	13	1960–69, 71–73
Bob Cousy	Boston	13	1951–63

The Top Scorers Each Year

		Team	Total Points	Average (per game)
1975–76	Bob McAdoo	Buffalo	2,427	31.1
1974–75	Bob McAdoo	Buffalo	2,831	34.5
1973–74	Bob McAdoo	Buffalo	2,261	30.6
1972–73	Nate Archibald	Kansas City	2,719	34.9
1971–72	Kareem Abdul-Jabbar	Milwaukee	2,822	34.8
1970–71	Kareem Abdul-Jabbar	Milwaukee	2,596	31.7
1969–70*	Kareem Abdul-Jabbar	Milwaukee	2,361	28.8
1968–69	Elvin Hayes	San Diego	2,327	28.4
1967–68**	Dave Bing	Detroit	2,142	27.1
1966–67	Rick Barry	San Francisco	2,775	35.6
1965–66	Wilt Chamberlain	Philadelphia	2,649	33.5
1964–65	Wilt Chamberlain	Philadelphia	2,534	34.7
1963–64	Wilt Chamberlain	San Francisco	2,948	36.9
1962–63	Wilt Chamberlain	San Francisco	3,586	44.8
1961–62	Wilt Chamberlain	Philadelphia	4,029	50.4
1960–61	Wilt Chamberlain	Philadelphia	3,033	38.4
1959–60	Wilt Chamberlain	Philadelphia	2,707	37.6
1958–59	Bob Pettit	St. Louis	2,105	29.2
1957–58	George Yardley	Detroit	2,001	27.8
1956–57	Paul Arizin	Philadelphia	1,817	25.6
1955–56	Bob Pettit	St. Louis	1,849	25.7
1954–55	Neil Johnston	Philadelphia	1,631	22.7
1953–54	Neil Johnston	Philadelphia	1,759	24.4
1952–53	Neil Johnston	Philadelphia	1,564	22.3
1951–52	Paul Arizin	Philadelphia	1,674	25.4
1950–51	George Mikan	Minneapolis	1,932	28.4
1949–50	George Mikan	Minneapolis	1,865	27.4
1948–49	George Mikan	Minneapolis	1,698	28.3
1947–48***	Max Zaslofsky	Chicago	1,007	21.0
1946–47	Joe Fulks	Philadelphia	1,389	23.2

*Best average per game 1969–70: Jerry West, Los Angeles, 31.2
**Best average per game 1967–68: Oscar Robertson, Cincinnati, 29.2
***Best average per game 1947–48: Joe Fulks, Philadelphia, 22.1

Field Goal Shooters

Most Field Goals

		Team	Made	Attempted	Average	Season
Career	Wilt Chamberlain	Philadelphia	12,681	23,497	.540	
	Oscar Robertson	Cincinnati	9,508	19,620	.485	
	John Havlicek	Boston	9,387	21,430	.438	
	Jerry West	Los Angeles	9,016	19,032	.474	
	Elgin Baylor	Los Angeles	8,693	20,171	.431	
Season	Wilt Chamberlain	Philadelphia	1,597	3,159	.506	1961–62
	Wilt Chamberlain	San Francisco	1,463	2,770	.528	1962–63
	Wilt Chamberlain	Philadelphia	1,251	2,457	.509	1960–61

		Team	Made	Attempted	Average	Game
Game	Wilt Chamberlain	Philadelphia	36	63	.571	vs. New York, Mar. 2, 1962
	Wilt Chamberlain	Philadelphia	31	62	.500	vs. Los Angeles Dec. 8, 1961
	{ Rick Barry	Golden State	30	45	.667	vs. Portland, Mar. 26, 1974
	{ Wilt Chamberlain	Philadelphia	30	40	.750	vs. Chicago, Dec. 16, 1967

Best Field Goal Percentage

		Team	Percentage	Attempted	Made
Career	Kareem Abdul-Jabbar	Milwaukee	.545	12,515	6,816
	Wilt Chamberlain	Philadelphia	.540	23,497	12,681
	Walt Bellamy	New York	.516	15,340	7,914
	Terry Dischinger	Detroit	.506	6,836	3,457
	Rudy Tomjanovich	Houston	.503	6,815	3,427

		Team	Percentage	Attempted	Made	Season
Season	Wilt Chamberlain	Los Angeles	.727	586	426	1972–73
	Wilt Chamberlain	Philadelphia	.683	1,150	785	1966–67
	Wilt Chamberlain	Los Angeles	.649	764	496	1971–72

Most Consecutive Field Goals

	Team	Total Made	Season
Wilt Chamberlain	Philadelphia	35	1966–67

KAREEM ABDUL-JABBAR

The Free Throw Shooters

Most Free Throws

		Team	Made	Attempted	Average	Season
Career	Oscar Robertson	Cincinnati	7,694	9,185	.838	
	Jerry West	Los Angeles	7,160	8,801	.814	
	Dolph Schayes	Syracuse	6,979	8,273	.844	
	Bob Pettit	St. Louis	6,182	8,119	.761	
	Wilt Chamberlain	Philadelphia	6,057	11,862	.511	
Season	Jerry West	Los Angeles	840	977	.860	1965–66
	Wilt Chamberlain	Philadelphia	835	1,363	.613	1961–62
	Oscar Robertson	Cincinnati	800	938	.853	1963–64

		Team	Made	Attempted	Average	Game
Game	Wilt Chamberlain	Philadelphia	28	32	.875	vs. New York, Mar. 2, 1962
	Frank Selvy	Milwaukee	24	26	.923	vs. Minneapolis, Dec. 2, 1954

OSCAR ROBERTSON

BUCKS
1

Best Free Throw Percentage

		Team	Per-centage	Attempted	Made	Season
Career	Rick Barry	Golden State	.890	3,120	2,778	
	Bill Sharman	Boston	.884	3,557	3,143	
	Calvin Murphy	Houston	.875	2,248	1,967	
	Mike Newlin	Houston	.858	1,707	1,465	
	Larry Siegfried	Boston	.854	1,945	1,662	
Season	Bill Sharman	Boston	.932	367	342	1958–59
	Rick Barry	Golden State	.923	311	287	1975–76
	Bill Sharman	Boston	.921	228	210	1960–61

Most Consecutive Free Throws

	Team	Total Made	Season
Calvin Murphy	Houston	58	1975–76

The Rebounders

Most Rebounds

		Team	Total	No. of Games	Average Per Game	Season
Career	Wilt Chamberlain	Philadelphia	23,924	1,045	22.9	
	Bill Russell	Boston	21,620	963	22.5	
	Walt Bellamy	New York	14,241	1,043	13.7	
	Nate Thurmond	Golden State	14,090	915	15.4	
	Jerry Lucas	Cincinnati	12,942	829	15.6	
Season	Wilt Chamberlain	Philadelphia	2,149	79	27.2	1960–61
	Wilt Chamberlain	Philadelphia	2,052	80	25.7	1961–62
	Wilt Chamberlain	Philadelphia	1,957	81	24.2	1966–67

		Team	Total	Game
Game	Wilt Chamberlain	Philadelphia	55	vs. Boston, Nov. 24, 1960
	Bill Russell	Boston	51	vs. Syracuse, Feb. 8, 1960
	Bill Russell	Boston	49	vs. Detroit, Mar. 11, 1965 vs. Philadelphia, Nov. 16, 1957

The Assisters

Most Assists

		Team	Total	No. of Games	Average Per Game	Season
Career	Oscar Robertson	Cincinnati	9,887	1,040	9.5	
	Len Wilkens	St. Louis	7,211	1,077	6.7	
	Bob Cousy	Boston	6,955	924	7.5	
	Guy Rodgers	San Francisco	6,917	892	7.8	
	Jerry West	Los Angeles	6,238	932	6.7	
Season	Nate Archibald	Kansas City	910	80	11.4	1972–73
	Guy Rodgers	Chicago	908	81	11.2	1966–67
	Oscar Robertson	Cincinnati	899	79	11.4	1961–62

		Team	Total	Game
Game	Guy Rodgers	San Francisco	28	vs. St. Louis, Mar. 14, 1963
	Bob Cousy	Boston	28	vs. Minneapolis, Feb. 27, 1959
	Ernie DiGregorio	Buffalo	25	vs. Portland, Jan. 1, 1974
	Guy Rodgers	Chicago	24	vs. New York, Dec. 20, 1966

NATE ARCHIBALD

Miscellany

Most Games Played

	Team	No. of Games	Seasons
Hal Greer	Philadelphia	1,122	1959–73

Most Consecutive Games Played

	Team	No. of Games	Seasons
John Kerr	Syracuse	844	1954–65

Most Playing Time

		Team	No. of Minutes	Seasons
Career	Wilt Chamberlain	Philadelphia	47,859	1960–73
Season	Wilt Chamberlain	Philadelphia	3,882	1961–62

Most Fouls

		Team	No. of Fouls	Seasons
Career	Hal Greer	Philadelphia	3,855	1959–73
Season	Bill Bridges	St. Louis	366	1967–68

Most Times Fouling Out

		Team	No. of Times	Seasons
Career	Vern Mikkelsen	Minneapolis	127	1950–59
Season	Don Meineke	Fort Wayne	26	1952–53

All Time Dream Teams

Before 1960

	Position	Player	Team
Offense	Guard	Bob Cousy	Boston Celtics
	Guard	Bob Davies	Rochester Royals
	Center	George Mikan	Minneapolis Lakers
	Forward	Joe Fulks	Philadelphia Warriors
	Forward	Dolph Schayes	Syracuse Nationals
Defense	Guard	Max Zaslofsky	Chicago Stags
	Guard	Bill Sharman	Boston Celtics
	Center	Bill Russell	Boston Celtics
	Forward	Paul Arizin	Philadelphia Warriors
	Forward	Tom Gola	Philadelphia Warriors
	Coach	John Kundla	Minneapolis Lakers

BILL RUSSELL

GEORGE MIKAN
BILL SHARMAN
BOSTON

DAVE DeBUSSCHERE
WALT FRAZIER
JOHN HAVLICEK

After 1960

	Position	Player	Team
Offense	Guard	Oscar Robertson	Cincinnati Royals
	Guard	Jerry West	Los Angeles Lakers
	Center	Wilt Chamberlain	Philadelphia Warriors
	Forward	Bob Pettit	St. Louis Hawks
	Forward	Elgin Baylor	Los Angeles Lakers
Defense	Guard	Jerry West	Los Angeles Lakers
	Guard	Walt Frazier	New York Knickerbockers
	Center	Bill Russell	Boston Celtics
	Forward	John Havlicek	Boston Celtics
	Forward	Dave DeBusschere	New York Knickerbockers
	Coach	Red Auerbach	Boston Celtics

BOB PETTIT

RED AUERBACH

Can do!
McAdoo!
Can do!
McAdoo!

HE CAN DO
JUST ABOUT
ANYTHING.

Can He Fly?